Original title:
The Emerald Room

Copyright © 2025 Creative Arts Management OÜ
All rights reserved.

Author: Giselle Montgomery
ISBN HARDBACK: 978-1-80581-840-3
ISBN PAPERBACK: 978-1-80581-367-5
ISBN EBOOK: 978-1-80581-840-3

Tranquil Corners of the Heart

In a corner where dreams play,
Laughter dances on bright foils,
Chairs topped with ice cream hats,
Where socks and sandals coalesce.

Chandeliers made of rubber ducks,
Giggling shadows on the wall,
Banana peels rug beneath our feet,
Unexpected slips that end in brawl.

Cupcakes whisper silly secrets,
Tickling ribs, the joy they bring,
Silly hats tip on our heads,
Like we're kings of jesters' spring.

There's a cat with a bowtie grin,
Winking at a fish in a hat,
A world where nonsense reigns supreme,
And hiccups cause a rhythmic spat.

Mirage of the Woodland Soul

In the woods where laughter hides,
Squirrels wear spectacles as they glide.
Rabbits play poker under the trees,
While owls call out, 'What's your tease?'

Mushrooms dance in polka dots,
Enticing fairies with their plots.
Branches make jokes about the fog,
While shadows trip over a lazy dog.

Cascades of Serene Vibrance

Waterfalls hum an old, sweet tune,
While fish wear hats that make them swoon.
A duck quacks out a clever chat,
As the sun beams down, making all that fat.

Colorful plants gossip like friends,
Each bud a secret, each leaf defends.
They giggle moistly under the sky,
As butterflies zoom and candidly fly.

Shades of Tender Growth

The leaves are painting with a wink,
While green beans chat about their stink.
Tomatoes roll on the garden floor,
As seasoned thyme tries to outscore.

Cabbages wear caps, like little kids,
Hiding from beetles in makeshift grids.
Bees hold court, buzzing with flair,
While chalk marks signal an outdoor fair.

The Allure of Smooth Emeralds

Gemstone bugs strut with a gleam,
In a world where everything's a dream.
They polish their shells with great delight,
Telling tales of their shimmering flight.

Marbles roll with antics bold,
In the treasure chest, stories unfold.
Sprightly adventures in every hue,
And giggles echo in playful view.

Oasis of Enchantment

In a corner so bright, where shadows dance,
Laughter leaps forth, given the chance.
Chairs knitted with dreams and tales untold,
The air thick with jokes, and hearts brave and bold.

From ceiling to floor, a kaleidoscope glare,
Strangers become friends, in this whimsical lair.
A teapot with secrets, spills tales galore,
While winks and broad grins sneak in through the door.

Verdant Echoes

In a garden of giggles, where whimsy grows,
Petals of laughter in comical rows.
Grass tickles toes, as the sun plays the fool,
Birds chirp in puns, while they gather at school.

A breeze replays jokes that the daisies once knew,
Each leaf whispers punchlines, just to tease you.
In this green haven, you're never alone,
For even the stones have a playful tone.

Emerald Enigma

Mysteries swirl like smoke in the air,
With mischief afoot, everywhere.
A cushion that giggles when sat on in jest,
And curtains that flutter, because they're possessed.

Each corner reveals a trick up its sleeve,
With riddles and laughs in a whimsical weave.
So come share a chuckle, don't be a grump,
In this puzzling place where realities clump.

The Hidden Refuge

Behind painted walls of vibrant delight,
Resides a nook that's a pure, silly sight.
Where the scones have costumes and tea never spills,
And laughter erupts, like wild, playful thrills.

This cozy retreat hums with charm and cheer,
With whispers of laughter that tickle the ear.
So take a seat here, let your worries rescind,
In a sanctuary where joy is the trend.

Between the Leaves of Time

In a jungle of vintage hats,
Lemons danced with silly cats.
Time stood still, with giggles loud,
As turtles formed a wobbly crowd.

A clock with legs began to prance,
As ants engaged in a wild dance.
Through the leaves, a whisper flew,
'What's for lunch? A shoe or two!'

Reveries of a Shimmering Retreat

In a realm where shadows peek,
Frogs debate who sings more sleek.
Moonlight tickles the silly air,
While rabbits strut without a care.

A waterfall of jellybeans,
Casts reflections of silly scenes.
Dancing ducks in fancy shoes,
Invite all guests to share their blues.

The Allure of Verdancy

Vines dressed in polka dots,
Holding meetings with the pots.
Squirrels in tuxedos, oh so bright,
Plotting cakes for a midnight bite.

Beneath the moss, a secret door,
Leads to snacks and much, much more.
Laughter bubbles like a stream,
In this quirky, leafy dream.

A Pilgrim's Path to Enchantment

With a map made of pizza slices,
He trekked through fields of sweet devices.
A giant pea waved a hello,
As he danced with a friendly crow.

Bubbles floated on a breeze,
Tickling toes with joyful tease.
Each step felt like a silly game,
In a world that knew no shame.

Glimmers of Forgotten Wishes

In a space where dreams once danced,
Odd socks and twinkling lights pranced.
A table set for tea with gnomes,
Who chat about their tiny homes.

They sip on lemonade with glee,
While judging all who dare to be.
A weathered cat sings songs of yore,
To cheer the critters, none ignore.

Old wishes float like bubbles bright,
They pop and giggle with delight.
The chandeliers wear hats of cheese,
As laughter echoes, aiming to please.

Chasing the Serpentine Light

Curly beams that twist and tease,
A game of shadows in the breeze.
The rug whispers tales of old,
While mischief mingles with the bold.

We chase the glints that flicker fast,
In a labyrinth of dreams amassed.
A rubber chicken leads the way,
With jokes to brighten up the day.

A roaring joke, a giggling chase,
We tumble through this wacky space.
Where nothing's quite as it appears,
And laughter drowns out all the fears.

An Oasis of Colored Memories

In a realm where colors blend and twirl,
Each hue a tale, a curious swirl.
The walls are painted in laughter's tone,
As hats of fruit are brightly shown.

A jester juggles pies with flair,
While cats in capes leap high in air.
An oasis where dreams wear shades,
And silly symphonies serenade.

With every corner, laughter blooms,
In rooms adorned with fluffy grooms.
Pointy hats and wiggly toes,
In this wonderland, humor grows.

Echoes of the Verdant Abyss

In a jungle where the humor's ripe,
Banana peels create a type.
Of slippage, giggles, and quick retreats,
As frogs wear polka dots on their feets.

The vines are tangled in twisted jokes,
And tales of wise allied folks.
A parrot squawks a pun-filled song,
While monkeys dance, they can't go wrong.

With shadows low and spirits high,
We dive into the laughter spry.
Amidst the lush and leafy dreams,
Echoes of joy burst at the seams.

Enchanted Shelter

In a place where laughter grows,
Even the shadows strike a pose.
A tangle of cushions, oh so bright,
Makes every guest feel pure delight.

Bright pixies dance on ceiling beams,
Chasing after hilarious dreams.
Where even the drapes giggle loud,
And the tablecloths weave jokes proud.

The floor's a trampoline for the chairs,
Jumping high, ignoring all cares.
Cacti wear hats, much to our cheer,
While the walls whisper, 'Come sit here!'

Every corner hides a funny tale,
The clocks tick sideways, what a trail!
Giggles bubble in the air,
In this magical, silly lair.

Breath of the Celestial Forest

In a grove where trees wear silly hats,
Bunnies play chess with chatterbox cats.
The sunlight winks through leafy green,
Creating a scene that's just obscene.

A squirrel recites poetry on a branch,
While the flowers sway and frolic in their dance.
Mushrooms chuckle at passing clouds,
Awkwardly laughing, feeling quite proud.

Crickets debate on the stage of night,
A symphony forming, oh what a sight!
The stars twinkle with laughter and glee,
As shadows perform an unplanned spree.

What a place to lose track of time,
Every tick and tock is oh-so-prime.
In this haven of giggles and glee,
Nature invites us to come and be free.

Whispers of Glistening Green

In a lush hideaway, laughter unfolds,
As ferns share stories that never get old.
The vines chuckle, entwined in glee,
While frogs croak jokes from the top of a tree.

Butterflies flutter, a comedic ballet,
Swinging and looping, what a display!
As snails slide in, with quirky finesse,
Their slow-motion race a humorous mess.

Daisies gossip on the soft, warm ground,
While raindrops giggle without making sound.
A breeze tickles leaves, a playful jest,
Inviting us all to come and rest.

In every nook, there's fun to be found,
A world alive with chuckles around.
Here in the green, where joy is supreme,
Life's little wonders fit like a dream.

Secrets in a Jewel-Toned Haven

In a castle made of sparkling hue,
Laughter twinkles like morning dew.
A chandelier hums a merry tune,
While jesters dance underneath the moon.

Carpets whisper secrets of delight,
Bringing mischief from day to night.
Colors collide in a playful parade,
Where every room invites a charade.

Candles giggle, the flames tickle bright,
Chasing shadows into the night.
In corners, rubber ducks organize,
Silly meetings to strategize.

This vibrant space, a joyful feast,
With every giggle, we're feeling released.
A haven of laughter, sparkling and bold,
This jewel-toned delight never gets old.

Verdant Whispers

In a garden bright and peculiar,
Plants gossip like they know you.
The daisies tease the dandelions,
While the violets write their opinions.

A fern twirls with a foolish grace,
Even the sunbeams crack a smile.
A roguish beetle struts in style,
As if he owns this leafy place.

Nearby, the tulips have a scheme,
To start a club, they dream a dream.
Membership depends on a good laugh,
And a hat made from a raindrop's half.

With laughter ringing through the leaves,
The roses giggle, sharing thieves.
Each whisper from the grass, so spry,
Keeps the humor floating high.

Jewel of Solitude

Amidst the quiet, colors gleam,
A solo cactus starts to scheme.
He rolls his eyes at passing flies,
And lays back down for a long sigh.

In sunlight's warmth, it seems he's shy,
Yet hides his jokes with a sly eye.
The shadows dance on walls so tall,
Where pine cones play a game of ball.

The gnomes on shelves wear looks of glee,
As wisps of moss sip herbal tea.
Each pot and plant knows quite the tale,
About the crickets' late-night wail.

Just watch the ladybugs parade,
As laughter simmers in the shade.
You'd think that solitude's a bore,
But it's a laugh-fest to explore!

Secrets in Green Shadows

In dim-lit corners, secrets stir,
Where clever vines begin to purr.
The shadows cast a funny play,
As leaves engage in witty fray.

A wise old tree rolls up his sleeve,
And tells the others to believe,
That laughter hides in every crevice,
Like a squirrel wearing a princess dress.

The mushroom hats are bowing low,
To greet the ferns who steal the show.
With quirky roots that tap dance round,
Nature's joke, an unseen sound.

Each breeze brings giggles from the past,
In every rustle, jokes amassed.
So gather 'round and lend an ear,
To greens that crack the dullest cheer!

Enclave of Lush Dreams

In a realm where ferns delight,
Dreams take wing in the moonlight.
Lush fantasies swirl around,
Where playful creatures leap and bound.

The flowers wear a zany crown,
And toss their petals all around.
Each color sings a merry tune,
To tease the tumbleweed and moon.

The nightingale, with cheeky flair,
Offers laughs while floating in air.
With jasmine scent that fills the space,
Even the stars wear a smiling face.

As laughter echoes through the glade,
Every shadow plays a charade.
In this enclave of whimsy bright,
Fun's the treasure on this night.

Emerald Echoes of Bliss

In a room where laughter bounces,
Green walls giggle, charm denounces.
Cushions jump, they play a game,
While the tea pot spills its fame.

Laughter flows like sparkling streams,
Through the air, in silly dreams.
A dance of chairs with wobbly legs,
Whispers secrets, and playful pegs.

Frogs in hats bring comic glee,
Jumping 'round like they are free.
Dandelion wishes, floated high,
Tickle our hearts as they drift by.

In echoes bright, good times are spun,
Where every mishap is just plain fun.
The room wraps us in joy's embrace,
Creating smiles upon our face.

Visions of the Grotto

In a cave of green, what a view,
Mushrooms wearing hats, it's true!
Shadows dance like they're in a play,
While giggling fairies join the fray.

Rabbits wearing monocles strut,
Telling tales of the world's big glut.
A squirrel conducting woodland tunes,
Beneath the smiling, chuckling moons.

Each corner buzzes with silly sights,
Frolicking grass and ticklish heights.
Mermaids with giggles splash the floor,
As bubble baths bubble, who could want more?

In this grotto, where visions delight,
Where nonsense reigns and stars are bright.
Every moment's a whimsical ride,
In the forest where fun and mischief bide.

Comfort in Green Reflections

Amidst the green, we take a seat,
With cushions soft, oh, what a treat!
The walls hum tunes of joy and cheer,
As snacks appear from nowhere near.

Good vibes float like daisies in air,
Comfort and laughter without a care.
We sip on jokes, brewed fresh like tea,
With every chuckle, we feel so free.

The room's a canvas, painted in green,
Where silly antics are seen and keen.
A nacho-shaped cloud hangs with pride,
Offering snacks and laughter wide.

In comfy corners, we lounge and grin,
Sharing tales of our latest din.
In reflections bright, we find our muse,
Where fun and friendships shall never lose.

Luminescent Dreams of Nature

In the glow of the playful light,
Nature pranks and takes to flight.
Fireflies wearing tiny tuxes,
Hosting parties with squeaky duckses.

Butterflies with polka dot ties,
Flutter and giggle under blue skies.
Jumping jays join in the dance,
They prance around with a saucy glance.

A marshmallow cloud bobs with glee,
Filling our hearts with sweet old spree.
In this realm where wild things play,
Every whimsy finds its way.

With laughter ringing through the air,
Nature's jokers create a fair.
In luminescent dreams of cheer,
We find our funny, gather near.

Resting in Nature's Casbah

In the shade, a lizard grins,
While squirrels dance, they twirl and spin.
A cozy nook in leafy green,
Where every joke is felt, not seen.

The flowers giggle, petals sway,
As bees say 'Buzz' in their own way.
A garden chair, oh what a throne,
With cushions made from moss and bone!

A breeze arrives, it breathes a laugh,
Caressing trees on nature's path.
The sun peeks in with cheeky cheer,
And even rocks can crack a sneer!

So come and join this playful space,
Where every leaf wears a smiling face.
In this delightfully odd fleet,
Taking a break is quite the treat!

Glow of the Green Sanctuary

Amidst the greens, a glow so bright,
A firefly twinkles in the night.
The worms recite their rhyming schemes,
While frogs discuss their lofty dreams.

A path of moss leads to the fun,
Where shadows play and laughter's spun.
The trees wear crowns of leafy lace,
While mushrooms pop with silly grace.

Unruly vines that like to tease,
Wave hello with a gentle breeze.
In every nook, a story's found,
With giggles echoing around!

This sanctuary, wild and free,
Where nature's antics truly spree.
Join in the jest, don't be shy,
In the glow, we'll laugh and fly!

Harmony Between the Petals

In gardens bright, the colors clash,
Daisies shout, while roses flash.
With every hue, a funny fight,
To be the most, oh what a sight!

Butterflies boast of their best dance,
While pollen snickers, taking a chance.
A breeze brings giggles from above,
As petals flutter, whispering love.

Among the blooms, there's mischief rife,
Where daisies tease the bugs for life.
In tiny chats, they plot and scheme,
A floral world, a whimsical dream!

So let us laugh with every flower,
In this bright, silly, petal power.
For every color seeks to play,
In nature's choir, we'll sway all day!

Porcelain Feel of Leafy Whispers

In whispers soft, the leaves confide,
A secret party, nature's pride.
With porcelain petals all around,
It's the funniest place to be found!

The rabbits joke with a groovy hop,
While guarding silver birch, they stop.
In this realm of leafy moods,
Every giggle bursts in the woods.

The shadows shift, a dance begins,
With nature's quirks, oh what fun spins!
Among the branches, laughter flies,
As the mockingbird jokes and sighs.

So linger here, amongst the green,
Where every rustle's a hidden glean.
For in this porcelain sanctuary,
Life's a jest, wild and merry!

In Twilight's Emerald Embrace

In the twilight glow they dance,
With slippers made of leafy chance.
Laughter spills from every wall,
As mossy critters join the ball.

A frog in tie and shiny shoes,
Tells jokes that only he can choose.
The fireflies serve as the light,
While shadows giggle at the sight.

Crickets play the lively band,
While flowers clap their tiny hands.
A squirrel wearing a crown of leaves,
Sways to tunes that nature weaves.

In this realm of goofy cheer,
Where nothing's ever quite sincere.
They skitter, jump, and tiptoe 'round,
In the laughter-laden ground.

Caressed by a Greener Dream

Beneath a vine, a party brews,
With broccoli in fancy shoes.
The lettuce laughs, what a silly sight,
As taffeta clouds float out of sight.

A hedgehog in a bright blue bow,
Tells tall tales of how things grow.
The thicket shimmers with glee and cheer,
As gossip spreads with every deer.

Bouncing bunnies play a prank,
As mushrooms dance on the riverbank.
They do the tango with a wink,
In a dream where greens all sync.

And in this wacky, leafy place,
A dance-off takes a comical pace.
So raise a cup, let's toast and beam,
To life inside this verdant dream!

Shades of a Hidden Realm

Where shadows sprout legs and run,
And squirrels compete to see who's fun.
The daisies wink with petals bright,
As they whisper secrets out of sight.

A bumblebee dons a velvet hat,
Swaggers by like a cool old cat.
In corners where the sunlight fades,
The giggles echo in leafy glades.

A wise old owl, with a comical tone,
Sings ballads of his well-known home.
He hoots in rhythm, a quirky beat,
As shadows sway to their own sweet heat.

In this space of giggles and jest,
Where every leafy creature finds rest.
Dance here between the light and shade,
In the quirky realms that nature's made!

A Glimpse Between the Foliage

Peeking through the leaves so green,
A jest unfolds, like never seen.
A turtle with a top hat spins,
As laughter rises, the fun begins.

A parade of ants in a conga line,
With marshmallow floats, it's simply divine.
Each new turn brings glee anew,
As dandelions stand up for their cue.

A parrot cracks a joke on cue,
While butterflies cheer with wings of blue.
In this quirky, lush retreat,
The sounds of laughter can't be beat.

So come and join this leafy spree,
Where whimsy walks with majesty.
A glimpse into this world of fun,
Where frolic meets the setting sun!

Reflections in Jewel Tones

In a space where colors dance,
Laughter echoes, take a chance.
Shiny walls and wobbly chairs,
Disco balls that float in airs.

Vibrant greens and playful blues,
Where everyone has silly shoes.
Hilarity in every glance,
A jolly, vibrant, wiggly dance.

Kooky hats and wigs of gold,
Here, all stories must be told.
Glimmers spark in cheerful eyes,
Ticklish socks and cupcakes rise.

Wonders wait on every shelf,
A giggle shared, who'd think of self?
In this space, the joy's a bloom,
No one's left out in this room.

Tranquil Canopy

A jungle gym, a leafy crown,
Swinging llamas all around.
Sipping drinks with floating ice,
Pineapple hats? Oh, so precise!

Breezes blow with laughter's cheer,
Squirrels dance, there's nothing to fear.
Hide and seek with a playful cat,
Whose mischievous dance is where it's at!

Ticklish vines and bouncing balls,
Friendly echoes in the halls.
Joyful shouts and whistles tune,
Echo through the leafy bloom.

Laughter swirls like clouds on high,
As monkeys play and dreams fly by.
In this haven, free and grand,
Every giggle's simply planned.

Celestial Verdure

Beneath a sky of glittering mist,
Oddities nobody can resist.
Stars on sticks, and comets swirl,
Mirth and mischief give a twirl.

Dance with fireflies, spin about,
Laughter's echo, any doubt?
A tapestry of vibrant glee,
This place, it sets our spirits free!

With creatures prancing, oh so sweet,
A silly jig, a happy beat.
They serve up clouds on silver trays,
Tasty treats that light our days.

Under the moon's whimsical glow,
All our worries seem to go.
Every whisper brings a smile,
Stay a while in this magical aisle.

The Secret Garden's Veil

In a garden where whispers sing,
Teacups dance, oh what a fling!
Petals laugh and vines converse,
As crickets hum a funny verse.

Hidden paths that twist and play,
Where every creature has its say.
Sassy squirrels with bits of cake,
In this space, it's hard to fake!

Lily pads in sunlit beams,
Turtles share their silly dreams.
Frogs in tuxes croak their thoughts,
Wondrous giggles fill the plots.

So come along, escape the norm,
Join the frolic, feel the warm.
Behind the veil, the joy's in sight,
In this hidden realm of light.

Dappled Light and Folly

In dappled light, the shadows play,
A squirrel steals acorns in a bold ballet.
The flowers giggle, their petals bright,
While bees in tuxedos buzz with delight.

A toad on a log makes quite the scene,
Sporting a crown made of leafy green.
Laughter erupts from the chirping throng,
Nature's own choir, singing sweet and strong.

The breeze tickles noses, it dances with glee,
As ants carry crumbs, oh so seriously.
A hammock sways under the grand oak's arm,
Whispers of mischief, a silvery charm.

With each light step, there's a comedic twist,
Frogs choreograph leaps, you can't resist.
In this jolly glade, where folly takes flight,
Every day's laughter, a sheer delight.

Twilight in Green Halls

Twilight weaves through green-clad trees,
Where shadows stretch and sway with ease.
A hedgehog rolls in an acorn pile,
Declaring himself king, quite with a smile.

Fireflies flicker, a dance of the night,
While owls hoot comically, a silly sight.
Bats zoom past, in their caped disguise,
Chasing moths, oh what a surprise!

The creek gurgles, telling tales anew,
Of frogs in tuxedos and crickets too.
Leaves rustle softly, laughing with the breeze,
Whispering secrets among the trees.

As stars peek out, the mischief takes flight,
In this playful realm, everything feels right.
So join the fun, let worries depart,
In this twilight dance, we embrace the art.

Nurtured by Nature's Breath

Nature whispers softly, a giggle in the air,
The daisies dance and twirl without a care.
A butterfly stumbles, lands on a shoe,
Declares it a garden, a fine spot to view.

Worms wear their glasses, reading the soil,
Discussing the weather in jest, such a toil.
While ladybugs argue, on who's the best friend,
Debating their spots, does the fun ever end?

The breeze, a playful friend, tugs at the leaves,
Cycling through branches, in air it weaves.
Squirrels contend with acrobatic flair,
Competing for snacks in a comedic affair.

As dusk drapes down, the mirth is alive,
With laughter and cheer, we happily thrive.
In this haven of whimsy, where life we embrace,
Nurtured by nature, we all find our place.

Cloaked in Verdancy

Cloaked in green, the forest sways,
A comical play, in so many ways.
A raccoon dons a mask, looks quite the snob,
As hummingbirds gossip, in a flower blob.

Mossy carpets invite a jump or two,
While dragonflies twirl in a bright ballet too.
Each leaf is a canvas, nature's art so bold,
Tales of starlight, in whispers told.

A chipmunk juggles, with nuts and a grin,
Collecting applause from the critters within.
Where laughter is plenty, and trouble's a jest,
Nature's own humor, it knows how to zest.

As dusk falls gently, with stars peeking through,
The forest lights up with a whimsical view.
Cloaked in verdancy, everything's bright,
In this playful paradise, we dance with delight.

Within Nature's Glistening Heart

In a glade where fairies dwell,
The trees all giggle, oh so well.
Flowers dance in cheerful tune,
Beneath a bright, chubby moon.

A rabbit wears a polka dot,
His tail is fluff, quite a lot!
Squirrels scamper, sly and quick,
Stealing acorns, playing tricks.

The stream chuckles as it flows,
Tickling fish beneath it goes.
Birds above in quick debate,
Forget the time, it's getting late.

Nature holds a laugh so bright,
Turning sadness into light.
In this realm of whimsy's art,
Joy lives in nature's glistening heart.

Retreats in Nature's Embrace

At dawn, the bees begin to hum,
While lazy frogs do gently plumb.
A tortoise tries to win a race,
But naps instead in leafy space.

The wind plays tricks, a swirling jest,
Kites are tangled, oh what a mess!
Laughter echoes, trees a-shiver,
In this place where spirits quiver.

Picnics spill with crumbs and glee,
Ants march in for a banquet spree.
Nature's laughter fills the air,
With every thrill, we strip despair.

In retreat beneath the sun's soft glare,
We wiggle toes without a care.
In nature's hug, we sing and dance,
With silly tales, we take a chance.

A Chamber of Shimmering Dreams

Beyond the hills where echoes play,
Lies a space where giggles sway.
Clouds wear hats of fluffy cheer,
Whispering secrets for all to hear.

The sunbeams scatter, toss and gleam,
In this wild and silly dream.
Kangaroos in tuxedos prance,
Juggling acorns in a trance.

Stars at dusk, oh what a show,
Raccoons dance in a row below.
Nature's jesters, all aglow,
Invite us in, so let's not slow.

In chambers lit with giggles bright,
Adventures spark with pure delight.
A world where whimsy reigns supreme,
Holds wonder in each sparkling beam.

The Spectrum of Solitude

In quiet nooks where shadows laugh,
The trees play chess, a leafy craft.
Owl wearing glasses, smart as pie,
Writes down poems, oh my, oh my!

A hermit crab dons silver shoes,
While dancing ants express the blues.
The solitude feels like a jest,
With nature's quirks, we are blessed.

Whispers of wind share quirky tales,
As lizards bask on sunny scales.
Every rustle, a secret shared,
In the stillness, laughter's aired.

Amongst the blooms and softest sighs,
Solitude's a fun surprise.
With nature's charm, we hear the call,
In this realm, we laugh and sprawl.

An Escape to Leaf-Laden Splendor

In a realm of green and cheer,
Where squirrels throw a wild beer,
We danced with foliage all around,
While chasing shadows on the ground.

The sunbeam's tickle made us grin,
As flowers laughed at where we'd been,
With butterflies that wore crushed hats,
We played hopscotch with the fat cats.

A picnic spread, a feast so grand,
Till ants arrived to claim their land,
We swapped our treasures for their crumbs,
The forest echoed with our thumbs.

With laughter ringing through the trees,
We braved the tickles of the breeze,
In nature's giggle, off we flew,
In leaf-laden splendor, oh how we grew!

Serenade of Verdant Breath

A tune of rustling leaves so bright,
With frogs composing rhythm slight,
The sunshine strummed a golden chord,
While daisies danced, oh how they soared!

The breeze would wink, a playful tease,
As crickets chirped with utmost ease,
A serenade of giggles flowed,
In this green stage, delights bestowed.

We twirled with roots, a dancer's grace,
Spinning tales in this lovely space,
The laughter echoed, sweet and clear,
With blossoms blooming, drawing near.

So join this jolly, leafy tune,
Beneath the sun, beneath the moon,
Where mirth and nature intertwine,
In the verdant breath, we sip divine!

Meetings in Glade and Gloom

In shadows deep, the critters scheme,
They plot and plan, a funny dream,
With rabbits wearing fancy hats,
While raccoons steal the potted plants!

A gathering where silliness reigns,
With thickets full of cheerful trains,
The owls gave sage advice in jest,
While sipping tea, we took a rest.

The bushes whispered silly puns,
As fireflies danced, oh what fun!
In glade and gloom, we're never shy,
With laughter soaring to the sky.

With every rustle, friendship blooms,
Among the laughter and the fumes,
In secret meetings, we unite,
In joy-filled shadows, day and night!

Glistening Pathways of Tranquility

A ribboned path of twinkling light,
Where giggles merge with soft twilight,
With every step, we dodge and weave,
In gentle hugs, we chose to believe.

The flowers winked as we walked by,
With petals sprinkling, oh so spry,
The ferns would chuckle, sing along,
In glistening pathways, we belong!

We skated on the dew-kissed grass,
With merry thoughts that came to pass,
While frogs held court and gave their vote,
On which funny hat we'd throw afloat!

With every breath, a joke was spun,
A silly world, oh how we run,
In pathways bright, old worries flee,
Our laughter echoes, wild and free!

Wandering through Verdant Dreams

In a place where green takes flight,
Laughter echoes, day and night.
With vines that wiggle, plants that prance,
Who knew ferns could join the dance?

A toadstool table, snacks galore,
I swear I saw a cycling spore!
Bumblebees in tiny hats,
Sipping nectar with the cats.

The leaves all whisper jokes untold,
As squirrels gamble with acorns bold.
While laughter sprouts from every bend,
Who needs a map? Just follow the trend!

In a world where whimsy grows,
And sunshine tickles, laughter flows.
So come on down, don't be a goon,
Join the frolic beneath the moon.

Oasis of Twinkling Hues

A patchwork quilt of colors bright,
Spinning tales of pure delight.
With crimson blooms and azure skies,
Where flowers gossip as they rise.

A rainbow bird with feathered flair,
Swings on branches, without a care.
Petals waltz in dazzling spins,
While ticklish grass tickles chins.

Marigold hats on daffodil heads,
Surreal dreams woven in threads.
Quirky critters sharing tea,
In a garden made for glee.

Bubbles float, dancing in air,
With every giggle, none can spare.
In this grove of twinkling glows,
Here's where the laughter truly flows.

Dance of the Lush Spirit

Mossy carpets, soft and bright,
Invite you in—oh, what a sight!
With shadows twirling, spirits play,
In this garden, joy's the way.

The ferns do shimmy, shake, and glide,
While pesky bees refuse to hide.
With polka-dot socks on a sleepy snail,
It's mischief day—let's set sail!

A giggling brook that sings all day,
Whispers secrets in its ballet.
The breeze joins in with a jest so sly,
As petals point and frolickers fly.

In vibrant hues, the party grows,
With every twist and turn it shows.
So waltz along this greenish spree,
Where nature's spirit sets you free.

Nature's Breathing Canvas

Canvas broader than the sea,
Doodles of life, so wild and free.
Rabbits sketching in the dew,
And the sun, a painter's hue.

With giggles from the leaves above,
And playful whispers full of love.
A canvas splashed with wacky shapes,
Chasing laughter through the drapes.

Squirrels posing like models neat,
In this gallery, none can beat.
Each bloom a brush of mischief bright,
Creating magic with pure delight.

So step right in, take in the view,
Where nature's heart paints all it drew.
With strokes of joy and bursts of cheer,
Join the masterpiece, my dear!

Shimmers of Nature

In a space where greens delight,
Laughter dances, taking flight.
Leaves wear smiles, branches sway,
Nature's chuckles on display.

Bugs play tag in sunny rays,
While flowers giggle in their ways.
An acorn rolled, oh what a sight,
As squirrels plot their nutty plight.

A lazy bee, in splendor hums,
It trips on nectar, oh, the bums!
With blooms adorned in joyful cheer,
Nature's jesters come right near.

So let's jump in, don't take it slow,
Join the fun, just let it flow.
In a world where silliness reigns,
Every green corner entertains.

Solitary Gem

In a nook where whispers roam,
Lies a quirky, plant-filled dome.
Its only friend, a grumpy fern,
Always waits for a great return.

Jokes collide amidst the leaves,
While daisies tease, growing thieves.
A lone chair sings of lazy tunes,
Beneath the watch of silly moons.

That spot where shadows play around,
Holds secrets in the leafy ground.
A lonely rock, with dreams so rare,
Tells tales of garden love affairs.

So sit a while and share a laugh,
With that old fern, your other half.
In this gem of solitude,
Life's so silly, yet so shrewd!

Lush Labyrinth

In a maze where colors burst,
The paths are wild, but never cursed.
With every turn, a joke unfurls,
As ribbons wave and laughter twirls.

Twisting vines, like playful kids,
Hide in corners, breaking bids.
A hedgehog's wiggle steals the show,
While creeping vines just want to grow.

Lost butterflies play hide and seek,
Amidst the giggles, nature speaks.
Each route a pun, a silly twist,
In this green maze, none can resist.

So skip along, don't take the map,
Join the fun in this leafy trap.
For every step, there's joy to find,
In this labyrinth where hearts unwind.

A Haven of Color

In a world that's painted bright,
Giggles echo, pure delight.
Each hue a tale, each shade a grin,
Where joy begins, and woes wear thin.

The reds and yellows hold a feast,
While blues sway softly, never ceased.
A dance of petals in the breeze,
Crafting joy with playful ease.

Fragrance frolics in the air,
Tickling noses everywhere.
A poppy winks, a sunflower bows,
It's a laugh-fest here—who knows?

In this haven, colors play,
Crafting smiles throughout the day.
Come for fun, stay for the cheer,
In this vibrant world, joy is near.

Tales from the Charmed Grove

In a grove where giggles bloom,
Squirrels wear hats, making room.
They dance on branches, swirl around,
Tickled by laughter, never a frown.

A frog in a tux jumps with flair,
Croaking tunes without a care.
Beneath the leaves, the fairies twirl,
As the breeze starts to give a whirl.

Mushrooms form a comedy club,
Where insects jive and bugs all rub.
A party of clowns, so quite absurd,
Each friend a joker, not one disturbed.

With each tickle, the trees giggle,
And branches shake, the leaves wiggle.
In this realm, the laughter flows,
Forever bright where charm bestows.

The Enchantment of Lush Serenity

In a vibrant patch of green delight,
Where hummingbirds play tag in flight.
A rabbit with shades sips tea,
Chatting with bees, oh what glee!

Beneath a sunbeam, a turtle dances,
Weaving in and out of lush glances.
He tells of days filled with fun,
While teaching ants how to run.

A picnic held by mushrooms wide,
Where potato salad takes a ride.
With forks and spoons all in a row,
Eating delights as the sweet breeze blows.

The grass holds secrets of laughter shared,
With each new jest, none unprepared.
In this scene, the joy won't cease,
For every creature finds their peace.

Veiled in Celadon Light

In a world bathed in lush green glow,
A smiling cabbage begins to show.
Carrots tell tales, quite funny,
Of dancing in the sun, bright and sunny.

Potatoes roll like bowling balls,
Chasing each other down the halls.
With giggles echoing through the shade,
As radishes prance, their jests displayed.

Beneath the sky of pastel hue,
A butterfly painted, turquoise and blue.
It flutters past, with a wink and cheer,
Leaving behind a trail of jeer.

In this serene grove of delight,
The sun waves goodnight, bidding goodnight.
With every chuckle, the blossoms bloom,
Joyful whispers fill every room.

Harvest of Greener Blessings

A garden where the peas all chat,
Debating which is fancier, the cat.
Tomatoes giggle, sharing tales,
Of sneaky squirrels raiding their scales.

Pumpkins roll in a game of tag,
Happily bouncing, never a drag.
Onions cry, but not from sorrow,
They join the pranks of a new tomorrow.

Corn on the cob sings in the breeze,
While peppers dance with utmost ease.
They laugh at clouds that try to rain,
Holding their joy, they'd never complain.

In every corner, humor thrives,
Each veggie plots joyful lives.
So raise a glass of veggie cheer,
To a harvest blessed with laughter here.

Threads of a Leafy Dream

In a garden of whims, where shadows dance,
Leaves giggle and sway, caught in a trance.
A butterfly slips on a banana peel,
And kisses a rose, oh what a deal!

The daisies all wear their best sunny hats,
While squirrels play tag and dodge acrobats.
The sun throws confetti, the breeze plays a tune,
While a frog tries to croak, but just hums to the moon.

Rains come and tickle the roots below,
As plants tell tales of their life's ebb and flow.
A snail starts a race, but he goes slow,
Yet all of us cheer, "You're winning, you know!"

An owl flips a pancake, oh what a sight,
With syrupy clouds that drip golden light.
In this leafy domain where laughter is found,
Imagination blooms and our joy knows no bound.

A Portal through Nature's Veins

Through twisted branches, a path leads on,
Where mushrooms blush at the break of dawn.
The ants hold a party with tea and sweet cakes,
While a hedgehog juggles the fruit that he makes.

The flowers all gossip, petals aflutter,
Sharing the latest, and oh what a clutter!
A fox in a top hat, oh what a scene,
Dances with shadows, it's fit for a queen!

The pond plays tricks with its mirror-like glance,
Where fish wear their best, ready to prance.
The lily pads giggle at frogs in a race,
While a raccoon takes selfies, strike a pose with grace.

All nature's delights merge in whimsical ways,
Creating a tapestry of sunny days.
Join this wild realm where silliness reigns,
And laughter is woven through nature's veins.

Serengeti of the Mind's Eye

A safari of thought, on wild winds we soar,
Where giraffes wear tutus, and lions roar more!
The zebras are dancing in polka-dot socks,
As monkeys zoom past, playing maracas like clocks!

A cheetah in shades sips a fruity delight,
Exchanging high fives with a kite in mid-flight.
While elephants trumpet tunes with great flair,
And rhinos in bowties twirls dance in the air.

Imagination gallops on vibrant bright plains,
Where the humor of nature completely constrains.
A hippo writes poetry in mud with a pen,
Signing all his work, "Love from the den!"

In this wild theater, every critter's a star,
With laughter resounding, both near and afar.
So grab your safari hat, let joy be your guide,
In this whimsical world where fun still resides.

Unraveling Tides of Nature's Jewel

As waves tickle shores with a playful embrace,
Seagulls do ballet, with grace and with pace.
An octopus tips its hat, ready to dine,
While crabs hold a banquet, all set for a vine!

The jellyfish glow with winks and with charms,
Inventing new dances with seaweed's arms.
A fish pulls a prank, hides under a rock,
And laughs as the dolphin says, "What a shock!"

The tide rolls in, with adventures to share,
A treasure chest bursting with laughter and flair.
But watch for the clam that might steal the scene,
With pearls of wisdom tucked snug in its sheen.

In this watery wonderland, smiles never cease,
As nature's own jesters bring joy and peace.
So dive into fun, let your spirit unfurl,
In the tides of hilarity that twirl and swirl.

A Prism of Earth's Unseen Blessings

In a space so bright and green,
Where laughter dances, seldom seen,
Jellybeans grow from every seam,
And giggles float like wisps of cream.

Bouncing balls of fluffy fluff,
A trampoline made of silly stuff,
Marshmallow clouds drift with delight,
Tickling toes by day and night.

Peeking through the shades of glee,
A merry parade of jubilee,
Singing songs of sweet surprise,
Where even the grumpiest smile wide.

In this land, joy's the only law,
Sharing smiles, holding back guffaws,
With each twist, a quirky embrace,
As laughter fills this silly space.

Shadows of Form and Light

Here shadows play a cheeky game,
Turning every frown to fame,
The cat wears glasses, quite absurd,
While bubbles float like whispered words.

Chairs start dancing, shoes take flight,
Colors spin and twirl with might,
A pickle juggles, trying its best,
While giggles bubble up with zest.

Light and shadow, a playful pair,
Knock-knock jokes float in the air,
Mirthful whispers, wise remarks,
As stories light up dreamy parks.

In this land of winks and charms,
Every oddity has its balms,
Curated chaos, joy intertwined,
As laughter echoes, truly kind.

Spirals of Green Enchantment

In a whirl of green, quite surreal,
Silly squirrels in hats of teal,
Bouncy sprouts laugh as they bloom,
With every twist, they brighten the room.

Twirly vines play peek-a-boo,
Dancing like a laugh, so true,
Dandelions tickle the moon,
Sending giggles to the tune.

The laughter flows like a stream,
Tripping on each joyous dream,
Grasshoppers cracking jokes on the fly,
Under the watchful, twinkling sky.

In this spiraled glee and cheer,
A bubble pops and sings the clear,
Unseen charms in every nook,
As fun unfolds like a storybook.

Serpentine Glimmers of Peace

In a corner where giggles gleam,
A serpent coiling like a dream,
Whispers of joy chase shadows away,
As chocolate chip cookies join the play.

Hopping frogs hold tiny crowns,
While laughter drowns most frowns,
Wiggly stars dance on the floor,
As everyone wants just a bit more.

In corners filled with stitches of light,
We build a world that feels just right,
With every chuckle, peace does seep,
As we twirl in fun, discovering deep.

Here, in glimmers soft and sweet,
Every moment feels so complete,
Embracing warmth in a fun retreat,
Where laughter and love like rivers meet.

Moonlight on an Abundant Canvas

In a land where colors gleam,
Everything's like a silly dream.
The daisies dance with tiny shoes,
While the grass giggles with the blues.

A tree wiggles, starts to sway,
As if to say it's time to play.
The moon whispers a cheeky tune,
Inviting all to join the boon.

Frogs are croaking jokes so bright,
While fireflies flash with sheer delight.
In this patch, laughter reigns supreme,
Nature's canvas—a funny theme.

With each brushstroke, joy unfolds,
A tale of whimsy, boldly told.
Using hues of green and gold,
In magical laughter, we behold.

The Green Interlude

In fields of green, the pranks unfold,
Where ants wear hats, so bold, so old.
A bumblebee with mismatched socks,
   Buzzes past the laughing rocks.

A snail with shades, on a sunny ride,
Said, "Life's a cruise, come join the glide!"
While daisies chuckle, heads held high,
   As birds crack jokes in the sky.

With each laugh, the sun grows bright,
And all the flowers join the fight.
In vibrant green, the world's a jest,
Where giggles linger, never rest.

From thickets' depths, the fun erupts,
A jolly tune, the forest interrupts.
Here in the green, we find our heart,
That's where the laughter gets its start.

Hidden Groves of Promise

In secret woods where giggles hide,
A squirrel prances with foolish pride.
Mushrooms wear a silly grin,
Inviting all the mice to spin.

The ferns wave flags of silly cheer,
Echoes of laughter linger near.
Clouds join in, roll up their sleeves,
As sunbeams shine on little leaves.

A tiny frog plays a banjo well,
While crickets join to cast their spell.
With every croak and every tune,
The hidden grove feels like a boon.

In this nook, mirth takes flight,
Where every moment is pure delight.
A dance of joy, so light and free,
In nature's heart, we find the key.

Spheres of Nature's Embrace

In circles drawn by emerald grace,
Stones and shells all find their place.
A toadstool stands, a throne of laughs,
Where bugs tell tales of daily gaffes.

The vines stretch out, a cozy hug,
Like a warm quilt, all snug as a bug.
Breezes giggle through the trees,
As playful whispers float with ease.

Each leaf's a note in nature's choir,
Perfumed with mischief, never tire.
As laughter rolls like a running stream,
In every heart, a shared daydream.

From playful roots to leafy skies,
In spheres of fun, our spirit flies.
With every chuckle, joy we trace,
Inside this sweet, green, timeless space.

Crystals of Life's Palette

In a room where colors dance,
Little gems frolic like a chance.
One says, "I'm the brightest star!"
But the green one laughs, "You're just bizarre!"

Canvases stretched and draped with glee,
Where splashes of joy meet the happy spree.
A painter's brush tickles the air,
Yelling, "Who knew art could be so rare?"

The blueberry shimmies, the cherry spins,
Mischief abounds where laughter begins.
"Let's throw a party!" the purple screams,
While the canvas winks and dreams silly dreams.

A splash of paint, a brush of cheer,
Forging memories year after year.
With every hue that dares to swoon,
Who needs the sun when you've got a tune?

Temptation in Leafy Whispers

In leafy lanes where gossip flows,
Squirrels chatter, and mischief grows.
"Did you see that acorn roll?"
"I've got two; let's barter for a stroll!"

Under the trees, where shadows flirt,
The mushrooms giggle in their dirt.
A deer peeks in with a wink so sly,
"Who knew leaves could party? Oh my, oh my!"

The bushes sway, a dance extravaganza,
Where the rustling leaves form a wild bonanza.
Petals flutter, giving it a try,
While the breeze jokes, "Am I just a fly?"

A chorus of colors, whirling around,
Nature's whimsy, where joy is found.
Don't mind me; I'm just leafing through,
Stumbling on wonders painted ay green and blue!

The Breath of Ancient Forests

Where ancient giants play peek-a-boo,
The forest whispers secrets to you.
A bark-toting owl hoots with glee,
"Man, I've lived longer than any tree!"

Ferns flutter by in graceful pirouettes,
Chatting sweet nothings, making bets.
"I once showed a piper how to dance!"
Leaves shimmy and sway, oh what a chance!

The mossy patches plot within,
A conference held where mushrooms grin.
"Bet you five acorns that squirrel will fall!"
Sure enough, he tripped over nothing at all!

With every snap and every crack,
The woods are quirky—no sense to lack.
Join the merry laughter in the pines,
In the realm of whispers, joy defines!

Imprints of Color Beneath the Sky

Under skies where laughter peeks,
A canvas sprawls, and magic speaks.
Clouds play tag, and the sun jests,
"Hey, your rays? Don't take a rest!"

The grass rolls green with playful delight,
Dandelions giggle, gripping tight.
"Blow, little seeds! Make your own trend!"
They drift like wishes, soft dreams suspend.

A butterfly enters with a wiggle and twirl,
"Hold your breath, for here comes the swirl!"
Colors collide, in a dizzy ballet,
Nature's art show, come join the fray!

Through every hue, a chuckle ignites,
In the gallery of day, where whimsy invites.
So let's frolic beneath this vast array,
For in these imprints, joy finds a way!

Reflections in Verdant Shadows

In a corner of jolly green,
A feathered friend appears unseen.
He's wearing socks—what a sight!
Laughter dances, taking flight.

A cat in shades, so suave and neat,
Is plotting quite a crafty feat.
It chases bugs with style and grace,
While giggles fill the silly space.

The plants gossip, whispering low,
"Did you hear? The goldfish stole the show!"
They wiggle and sway, having their say,
As laughter blooms in merry display.

What tales these leaves could share all day,
Of mischief found in bright array.
With every chuckle, joy ignites,
In shadows draped with leafy lights.

A Sanctuary of Lush Dreams

In a cozy nook where sunbeams play,
A squirrel dons a beret for the day.
He scurries left and darts to the right,
Creating chaos, what a delight!

A turtle rehearses a dance with flair,
While the blooms chuckle, losing their hair.
"Twirl around!" the daisies cry,
As butterflies twirl in the sky.

The gnome on the shelf with a wink and grin,
Sips tea with a ladybug, what a win!
They laugh at the time, so whimsically spent,
In this jolly spot, where joy is lent.

Every shadow holds a playful jest,
A home for laughter, a cozy nest.
Here, dreams bloom like flowers so bright,
Under the sun's warm, cheerful light.

Tapestry of Enchanted Hues

A canvas bright, with colors that sing,
Where every petal wears a shiny ring.
The bees buzz jokes, as they flit about,
Creating chuckles, without a doubt.

Goldfish wear hats, oh what a scene!
"Let's start a band!" they all convene.
The bubbles rise, as joy takes its cue,
In this lively place, where dreams come true.

Vines tangle with laughter, a playful tease,
In corners where mischief sways in the breeze.
With every tickle of sunshine's embrace,
Joy dances freely, filling the space.

A tapestry woven with giggles and cheer,
Where the magical whispers are always near.
Colors burst forth, like confetti in flight,
In this delightful realm, hearts feel light.

Beneath the Canopy of Desire

Beneath a leafy arch, a secret blend,
Where each leaf offers a cheerful trend.
Stand by the fountain, hear the frogs croak,
As the chattering flowers begin to poke.

The sun winks down, sharing its glow,
While the mushrooms giggle, feeling the flow.
"Jump higher!" calls out a playful breeze,
As laughter spirals among the trees.

Dancing shadows, a playful charade,
Turn meanderings into grand parade.
And while the moon whispers a funny tune,
A sprawled-out cat claims the afternoon.

A cabaret of nature, vibrant and bright,
With comedy woven in the soft light.
In each nook and cranny, joy takes flight,
Beneath the canopy, everything feels right.

www.ingramcontent.com/pod-product-compliance
Lightning Source LLC
Chambersburg PA
CBHW070319120526
44590CB00017B/2748